PRISCILA UPPAL

BLOODAXE BOOKS

ISBN: 978 1 78037 117 7

First published 2015 by
Bloodaxe Books Ltd,
Eastburn,
South Park,
Hexham,
Northumberland NE46 1BS.

www.bloodaxebooks.com
For further information about Bloodaxe titles
please visit our website or write to
the above address for a catalogue.

Supported using public funding by
**ARTS COUNCIL
ENGLAND**

Cover design: Neil Astley & Pamela Robertson-Pearce.

Printed in Great Britain by Bell & Bain Limited, Glasgow, Scotland, on
acid-free paper sourced from mills with FSC chain of custody certification.

For all those who pick up the pieces
with bare hands

CONTENTS

FOOTNOTE

If we see light at the end of the tunnel, it's the light of an oncoming train.

ROBERT LOWELL

Because your crystal ball ain't so crystal clear

BEASTIE BOYS

ACCUSATIONS

Accusations

Summer nights ripe for accusations, I twirl my parasol
while you tip your straw hat to store fronts.

I accuse your briefcase of prematurely filing for bankruptcy.
You accuse my hairpins of setting fire to the toolshed.

I accuse your desk drawers of alcoholism.
You accuse my running shoes of adultery.

I accuse your grooming kit of harbouring dangerous fugitives.
You accuse my paperbacks of plagiarism.

I accuse your mother of sabotaging our cheese fondue.
You accuse mine of bugging our bedroom, exterminating our
transcripts.

I accuse your love of being small.
You accuse me of dumping mine on the side of the road
like a lame dog.

We accuse bowls of cold water at the doors of nursing homes
of debunking our seniors.
We accuse elevators of treason.

All this before the bullied sun offs itself.

The Responsible Party

The Dream knows best, and the Dream, I say again, is the responsible party.
DE QUINCEY

We wake on sand, whipping up fortresses from abandoned claws.
The moon a gold button on the blazer of night.
We bodysurf with the tide, wash hair with visions of ecstasy,
lose weight sliding down pyramids.

My father announces he has turned into a tradesman.
My mother that she will birth hundreds
of babies and teach them to sew.
I keep up my ceaseless pilgrimage.

A city takes refuge in my brain. Then academies.
I hold daily trials. My heart is a madhouse,
jewellery bartered for stars. Heads roll
and flags permit all sorts of indulgences.

My doubt takes a trip north and plants poppies.
Our songs become faster and more cynical.
I've almost forgotten what sand tastes like when it sticks to mouth,
where the sun shines in the grand scheme of things.

Missiles, hand grenades, and hot air balloons lampoon
in the mountains. Rivers run green and drink vacations.
I'm famished and worried about dissolving towers.
My dream once lived here. It fled the riots, but

has forgotten how to breathe underwater. I blame not
the sky or the incompleteness of historical continuity.
I blame our eyes, our toes, our pitiful cities, and
the arcane mischief we conspire in our sleep.

A Diorama of Your Anger Drifts Downstream

It's not in a rush; heavy, plump,
invites the splash of water on skin, mud
on frame; builds speed
in time.

Your anger has built a raft, a life jacket,
scuba diving equipment. This anger
goes deep & turns exotic colours. Parts
of its species are yet to be
catalogued.

To onlookers: the ordinary calculated
occurrence of aberration, deviation
from an outside temperature gauge.
Coke can or olive branch, a tag off
a teenager's sweater, a plastic lunch bag.

Sometimes fishermen bait you,
then throw you back.
Elusive fame.

Continental drifting. Rumours
study maps of the falls,
then enflame.

Ancient men sing songs of grief.
You drag their notes along.

Class Action Suit

I am urging you to join my class action suit –
already millions strong – suing the fine arts for centuries
of criminal negligence resulting in countless occurrences
of inoperable emotional suffering.

If you've ever felt offended, or discomfort, or indigestion,
a pang of nostalgia, regret, boredom from a work of art – be it
a sculpture, an aria, a monologue, or a line of poetry –
do not be afraid to make your abuse known to your victimiser.

We are better than this force of attack.
Strength in numbers. In truth.
Art has acted as a closed circle, hiding its ulterior agenda
and perverse crimes from us for too long.

We must drag the bodies into the light.
And you may likely have been harmed by more than one
perpetrator. By someone you know. Add your name
to existing lists. William Shakespeare just eked past

Pablo Picasso and the Sex Pistols. Personally,
I'm not ashamed to tell you, I belong to three.
I'm confident we will wake to the dawn of a future without
Spielberg films, the Group of Seven, and *The Faerie Queen*.

I sympathise with how difficult it is to relive the trauma
by coming forward. Professionals are on hand to help
your transition and to connect you with fellow sufferers.
Just think of the compensation you've been denied.

No one deserves to live through this on their own.

The Police Came for a Visit

just as grandma used to drop by before
      her nervous breakdown & the stroke.
I laid out two pots of loose-leaf tea
      & a selection of wheat-free, dairy-free cookies.
They removed their boots & caps
      but looped their guns around their fingers
& joined me on the carpet where I taught them 2
      expert knitting stitches while they explained
clause 3.21 of the Search & Seizures Regulations.
      My bladder was full so they insisted on escorting
me & standing guard as I washed my hands
      with cranberry soap. We traded photographs.
Yes, yes, that's my uncle, I assured the tall one,
      no, no, he's not a doctor, he's a nurse.
The short one placed uncle in a special envelope.
      I put on a video while they napped &
napped & napped – why wouldn't they wake up?
      Just like grandma, I thought, to visit & leave
you to lift crumbs off your floor. I was looking
      forward to testing out the sirens & earning
a new badge, kissing their smooth cheeks & waving
      like a widow from the driveway.
The walkie-talkie won't stop bleating. In a few
      moments, after I finish combing their hair
I'll sing *happy birthday* to you to the dispatcher
      just like Marilyn Monroe.

Autumn

Wearing a smile or frown
God's face is always there
It is up to you
If you take your wintry restlessness into the town

P.K. PAGE, 'Autumn'

Devastating autumn, climb the tree in your orange
mood. Last year you believed in goodness the way a spider
believes in her web – patterned threads to trap the charms
of life. You thought there was a time to get together,
secure love like a bracelet around your wrist.
Kick at this season – leaves fall like dried brown
confetti. The mind plays havoc with your dress
and you are bare, bare as the limbs you crack
as you dare the fates to throw you to the ground
wearing a smile or frown

Only little girls are loved by God,
you once thought, forgetting that as a little girl you
were loved violently, spread like an orchid in terror
of white light, cold shivers that bump, bump up
in the closet space, bedroom corners, the changing
sheets of the year. Now you think it's not fair,
not fair at all that adults are left to fall like acorns
or apples, fathers like once-bitten angels, blood lust
and husbands and rage, awful eternal stares.
God's face is always there

Pleading '*mercy*, mercy on *me*, dear one,
I faltered once just as you, climbing this very tree
while the green was sucked from my sides, my face,
the nail in my forehead crushing wisdom into dust.'
And you trust Him again, in fear of failing yourself,
in fear of this season turning to dust of misjudged truth.

You pick leaves, find a hallway to call your own,
hold court with the flies and the fathers, husbands, and other
unmentionables crouched outside the window, yelling *shrew*,
it is up to you

Save the world. It's worth saving. You're in orbit
whether you like it or not. Cyclical as rain, as your city lights
blinking on and off, on and off. Your bruises
will heal. Your legs will stand. This is the fall to echo all falls,
so you slide your coat across the shaved nails of the tree's
fingertips, and dive inside the orange space until you drown.
Hands, more hands, like the suspicious clouds
close in. *Inside here? Inside here?*
God running amok, daring to rip your gown
if you take your wintry restlessness into the town.

A Fall from Grace

That's what Daddy said about
Gandhi and Pakistan – it was his fall
from grace. The Chosen One
had chosen wrong and left a fraudulent
flower trail. This was Daddy's lesson

on loyalty, I think. I was in grade four
and was wondering too hard what Mommy
was up to half an ocean away on holiday
using the same passport she had stolen
from the vault to fly out of here. Daddy

drank scotch in the sun that Friday and
ordered me to play ball on the opposite side
of the street – he needed room to think –
he never believed we wouldn't
have a woman around. He laid down

borders on the lawn with white tape
while my brother and I cut out paper
wings and held them against our backs
with clothes hangers. Then we burned
the curtains and the sheets. Don't waste

what's left, Daddy scolded. Pressed
his ear against the earth and swore he
heard it tremble. His eyes searching the sun's
harsh rays for the anticipated approach
of an unscheduled cross-country train.

Essential

My mother insists a purse
is a target for terrorists – a bomb
in every lap – credit cards
and drivers licenses, suicide notes.
(She's a pessimist, my mother,
and relies too heavily on
prescription medications.)

My retail friends inform me
the handbag has saved the over thirty-five
economy. Designer gear for old
and fat ladies, ready to wear
like invented happy memories.

When I need a bottle of shampoo or
condescend to ride transit or confront
my front door, I pat myself
for clues as to where my change
or token or key might be.

I've stored bills in my cleavage,
gift certificates in my socks. My vertebrae
is one endless grocery list. My skin
sighs, groans, sometimes cries a little
depending on the nature of the transaction.

I stopped carrying a purse
months ago, yet can't shake the feeling
I've forgotten something essential,
as if I could tote my heart about
in a basket, or sling my brain over
my shoulder and go for a long run.

In the Psych Ward

There are days I imagine you floating away
attached to the end of a black umbrella
lost among the black roaming clouds.

There are days I imagine you living solely off
scones & clementines, your ribs sticking out
like the wiry pickets of your thoughts' fence.

There are days I imagine you coughing yourself
out of happiness – the last unsalvageable vestiges
trapped like clogged arteries in your chest.

There are days I imagine you marrying a television
or outdated exercycle, doling out the day to day
like a maximum security death sentence.

There are days I imagine you reading a biography
of your alternate life, where you control the sun's
happenings by piercing the foil of your pills.

There are days I imagine you splitting your pajamas
your long white body an alabaster sculpture
for your fellow residents to draw.

There are days I imagine you muttering a choir
of complaints, baton in hand, the PA system bleating
between bars the arrival of code blue.

There are days I imagine you climbing the tower
of food trays and grey toiletry lockers like
a tropical gecko in search of perfect camouflage.

There are days I imagine you clicking the computer
mouse, silently sending your depression off
like the virus it is into the stratosphere.

There are days I imagine you kneeling in front
of the team of shifty doctors, receiving
on your shoulders the cold steel touch of knighthood.

There are days I imagine you settling into bed
in the afternoon like a little boy tuckered out with play,
that those alien notions are pucks rattling about your brain.

And there are nights I imagine me looking into your eyes
recognising the man who used to love me, as our days
get shorter, the way the span between holidays is longer

when you have nowhere else to be but here.

High Tide

My heart washed up on the beach.
Bloated like the Man o' Wars the posters
warned us about. A casualty of

the storm, I'd thrown it overboard,
convinced it would sink as I listened
attentively for its last petty bubbles

to fizz out, for the ocean to perform
its own cold blue burial rites, for slick
fish to carve out a coral reef. I motored

back to shore. Before sunset, the water
coughed up its lungs and there you
were again, bruised and soggy as always,

begging feebly for resuscitation. I played
Frisbee with the clouds while the locals
frantically shooed the children away

who strung your valves into necklaces.

The Dead Have Sabotaged My Facebook Page

Tampering randomly with logins and passwords,
eureka resulted in unlimited entry to my profile,
photos, and status updates. I am now five hundred
years old, single, and looking for that special someone
to 'love me two times'. Apparently, I am allergic
to green apples and can see through polyester.
Who knew the dead have a sense of humour?
Dropped Bert into my wedding, my kid's soccer team,
and the all-you-can-eat buffet in Cancun, Mexico.
Poked my mother, sent booty calls to coworkers,
and urged my high school reunion organiser to jump
naked out of a cake. A vicious bastard advocated suicide
to my stepbrother as the path to enlightenment.
One young woman – I know by the childish shorthand
and emoticons – writes endless epistles in Egret.
I have no idea who my contacts are: my list bloated to
the size of a small country. Pistols, parkas,
exercise equipment, herbs and sausages arrive by
the truck load. I get hate mail from celebrities
I've never heard of. I seem to owe money at every turn.
On my home page, I'm still smiling. And my cat videos
remain intact, but I have highly restricted access
to my thoughts and dreams. I could hear the screen
beeping up a storm last night, and barely slept from
all the chatter. Since when was death a social network?
Urgent Update: The planet's population has doubled.
I have no need for this many friends.

Union Guarantees Health Benefits into the Afterlife

A banner year for CUPE 3903
in a series of unprecedented victories
the union has strong-armed the employer
to fund birthday and anniversary parties,
cock and breast enlargements, social network activities,
and, as of midnight last night,
job security and medical benefits into the afterlife.

'We have God and his scabs right
where we want them,' Union Steward
told reporters. 'He knows we can overwhelm
those pearly gates and slow traffic to zero.
We have plenty of comrades undercover
erecting barricades.'

Other motions on the table in this 'next wave
of activism' include afterlife transsexual surgeries,
spousal disability claims, and workers' compensation.

'There's no reason anyone should be
forced to quit working because of a little mortality.
That's prejudice,' shouted one picketer.

Employee concessions include mandatory
hand-washing (provided they still have hands)
and no singing on the job. Both sides
agreed to punch the clock.

'Even if we're just sitting around
smelling the roses,
doesn't mean we're not entitled
to overtime.'

Compassion Fatigue

Jack has had enough
  of gang violence.
Samantha her fill
  of rape.
Justin's turned his back
  on the homeless.
Amrita hoards can tabs
  in her safe.
Han can't spoon another
  cup of cheer for the elderly.
Melissa can't sign another
  cast.
Peter refuses to grant
  cancer wishes.
Carter's underground railroad
  passed.

Jenny doesn't care if
  you're hurting.
Barb denies Kleenex
  when you cry.
Do you really care who will
  drop dead in my next poem?
I mean, really,
  do I?

Leaving Sarajevo

In the rain the city is shy.
Like a jilted lover from a bygone era it searches
the grey streets & cold alleyways, strolling
into every coffee shop for one who once was, ignoring
the off-colour jokes from sunrise to sunset, the laughter
of the minarets, as mothers warn children against
wet hair & ice cubes, the slightest drafts.

When it rains, it rains for eternity.
Forgiveness is not a noun or a verb, but a threat.
The clouds descend like luggage the ancestors
drag back to old haunts, pastry shops & leather
wares, the bridge of many names. Drenched
but determined, the past runs for cover.

This is a city with a sun stuck
in its throat.

DISCUSSIONS

Discussions Concerning Artistic Merit

1

Do you love sonnets?
I love line-ups.

2

The apple is round.
The pie is round.

The apple and the pie are equal in diameter.

Persephone declines to eat with a fork or spoon.

3

Do you love duets?
I love oxymorons.

4

Waking in the turbulent waters of the mass' consciousness
is like drifting on the eyelash of a planet.   Hold on

with tight fists, though you scorn the touch.   Though you'd
rather hear the ocean's aquarium than feed it.

Sand in ears. Golden mirages. Trees like   sticks of incense
burn, burn out. A forehead is a matter

of opinion.   Wipe it and   assume your pose.

5

Do you love the theatre?
I love assassinations.

6

Select a photograph:

In the third album you are still alive. Where are my gloves? you ask.
Or that boyfriend who liked to drive in the slow lane and eat pickles
for breakfast?
Why is his hair flaking off like pastry in my hands?
Where did my hometown bugger off to? Why has mother French-
braided my hair?
Am I fashionable? Anachronistic? A development?
Did he/she live on my street and skip rope or race ten-speeds?
Did she/he get assaulted with a car jack in the drugstore parking lot?

Remember August. Remember Clarinet. Remember Birthday
Streamers.

Apparently, I adored smiling. Who will remember me unhappy?
Who will drive in depression like some beat-up sports car and
hand over the keys?

I must not have wanted to remember father in his armchair rattling
on about the price of peas and potatoes or his sickly village back
home, must not have wanted to recall my first school girl crush or
track meets or stained shorts and hands on knees underneath
cheap plastic tables and bandstand stages.

I wished not for seasons to change, only for turning. Science
squelches sunrise into a less surprising affair. Science squashes
albums. Errors trapped within corners. Sometimes abortion

is merciful.

7

Do you love arches?
I love heels.

8

A viewer acrobats into algebra.

A line points to its own conclusion.

A dog barks up a wheelbarrow.

A dove soliloquies on the disquietude of branches.

9

Do you love the colour green?
I love bank statements.

10

We dream in five dimensions:

> This, admittedly, is a hypothesis. No factual data has currently been collected into a cohesive, intelligible, formula as of yet. Good luck with openings and closings. We are each awarded fifteen minutes in the centre of the universe. Lovers picnic on landmines. Perhaps you prefer paper dolls with heads cut off, surreptitious kleptomaniacs, a dungeon of mice. Real people die here, too. Are set on fire. Decapitated. Even children. Data demonstrates we rarely apologise for what we dream. We rarely apologise. For what? We...dream.

11

Do you love sonatas?
I love car alarms.

12

St Augustine believed time could exist only in heaven.

It is no wonder your mother wept
seeds of African sunflowers.

Fleeing her tent that night
you cowered in the corner
just like a philosopher or saint.
Belittled by belief.

Mother, if this is Time, you declared, *I will have none of it.*

Perspiring is the skin's kiss.

13
Do you love film reels?
I love vertigo.

14
Bludgeon the canvas.
Bleach the paper.
Blind the cameras.
Buffet the body.
Bend the bridges.
Boycott the orchestra.
Bankrupt the syllables.
Backstab the stage.

Beware the history of artistic movements.

15
Do you love stories?
I love morals.

ADAPTATIONS

Survivor

A millionaire is shot. And his wife. And their unborn child.
Revenge selects an arsenal of weapons.

Armies drawn by lots construct arguments.
Leaders rise like tanks and airplanes.
Gardens plant anxious roots.
Gossip punished by banishment.

Goodbye beautiful youths.
Perhaps you would like to marry a sweet blond or bouncy brunette
before the bullet rounds.
Perhaps you would like to use a lifeline to mail a letter
to your attorney, or ask your dear
old mother for advice.

Each week, ten thousand foot soldiers are served
faulty gas masks, ten thousand more must give up
their limbs for tent pegs.

The challenges get crueller. The prizes stranger.
The confessions more predictable.

Nations text their ballots into the trenches,
go back to genetically modified dinners
and genetically modified cares.

As soon as a commercial break calls truce,
the fan website nearly crashes from all the orders
for bright red poppies and T-shirts that read Never Forget.

Temptation Island

Henry keeps falling in love. What a problem!
What a hit among the lower classes!

A mob surrounds the coast's circumference
angling for a glimpse of a lace ruffle, the whiff of a cigar,
the sounds of string quartets or actors' monologues
for the aphrodisiac of courtship.

Gold, gold; palace sets all painted in gold.
Whole crews employed solely for the purpose
of spreading aristocratic fever.

Do you love me for my money or my charm?

The question wafts along the waters,
at times answered truthfully, at others submerged
under sugar cane and sapphires.

He must choose another wife. Or someone must die.

Behind his crown Henry smiles, nonplused,
having scripted this scenario before
after tasting half the lips of England.

Off with her head! Off with her head!

It's hard to say who leaked the information first.
Even before the episode aired, the cheer was catchy.

Cosmic Idol

Each week he must adopt a new style
and out-wit, out-sing, out-dance, out-ham his competitors.

The pace exhausting: early-morning and late-night rehearsals,
bickering of choreographers;

then the indignity to submit to the snarky British judge,
the washed-up diva, the pop producer with the three-word vocabulary,
and the schmaltzy commentary by the over-friendly host.

Orpheus curses how he got dragged into this business in the first place.
To attract an agent? Free publicity?
The chance to prove once and for all that, given the platform,
he could bring an entire planet to its knees?

How is it he's found himself in pancake make-up, fussing about his hair,
the cut of his jeans – how the fabric fits snugly around his classic ass?
Will he be hip with the kids? Down with the guys?
The bomb?

A musical score conducted by strobe lights.
Three-headed monsters guard the stage.

Was it a woman he was wooing?
An old friend with a chronic cough?
His childhood basset hound?

Behind the curtain, amid confetti, a shadowy figure calls to him.
Oh, please, he begs, *let it be my next hit song.*

Rehab with Dr Drew

Somebody please stop me.
Intervene.
Or I'll give myself up again.

I'm addicted to rehab.
To the physical place & psychological space.

I love the checking in & checking –
out. The throwing up & the grave
self-doubt.

I can't get enough doctors
& nurses & personal prayers &
self-actualising goals.

One day there will be altars,
monuments of Rehab.
Rehab votive candles &
Rehab celebrity trading cards.

I love tearing my heart out & eating it too.
I love counting foil packs and playing the fool.

Mark my words:
The Goddess of Rehab brings families and nations together.

Since she is old hat to me,
I'll escort you to your cell.
Better yet – let's be roomies.
There's so much to tell.

We've got a long, long wait
before we're cured.

The Amazing Race

I
Bored atoms leaning against dimensional walls
kicking up a fuss. Bang, bang.
Countdown to extinction.

II
Cave-dwelling couples copulate.
The continents begin bickering.
Rates of drift rise.

III
If you can get your hands on an accurate map,
you are so ahead of the game.

Doubly so if you are quick at picking
up languages. Or if you know someone famous
who will lend you a boat.

The trick is to plunder with purpose, land
agricultural punches, haggle
into power. (And kill Indians.)

If you can get your hands on sugar or coffee,
you are so ahead of the game.

IV
This episode, gods spread like lice.

Instead of cutting off the plague at the roots,
we attempt varieties of cleansing.

Next week, there will be fewer competitors,
but more puzzles and brain teasers.

    V

Finally, the arrival of guns.
Now the wolves will separate from the lambs.

    VI

Trade a Christian for a Muslim.
Trade a hooker for a doctor.
Trade a rickshaw for a parachute.
Trade a donkey for a Malamute.
Trade a prescription for an anthem.
Trade a watchtower for a bulldozer.
Trade a poem for a pendant.
Trade a bar stool for a bazooka.
Trade an orphan for an orgy.
Trade a human for a city.

Watch the stocks rise and fall.

    VII

If you are feeling homesick
rest assured you are not alone.
The vast majority of the planet
is nothing but a series of loungers
at the boarding gates of time.

    VIII

Thrill-seeking finds its own routines.
Press a button and old surges reinvent themselves.

IX

At his juncture, four out of five teams
are forced to apply for new passports.
Average wait times are anywhere from
five seconds to five lifetimes.
The world turns according to:
Lists. Lists. Lists.

X

After much fierce debate
(and thousands of ritual killings
plus other sanctioned bashings)
the legal definition of a couple is changed.

XI

If you can outwit diseases,
maximise resources,
purge toxins,
bank memoires,
pawn off your undesirables on the locals,
and have enough left in reserve
to sprint to the finish...
you can vanquish your enemies and
one day realise your dream
of owning a Cadillac
or opening a vegan restaurant.

XII

After all these legs and pitstops, fights and miscues,
(our fates forever entwined) how is it
we still don't have anything resembling a clue?

Toddlers in Tiaras

Once upon a time
in a land far far away
a King held a competition
to see which of his three daughters
loved him more.

I love you so much
I will grow up in a flash—
and be your loyal wife,
combing my hair and
painting my toes
only to your liking,
spraying myself
with sheer and silk.

I love you so much
I will never grow up –
never marry –
I will be forever and ever
twirling batons
bouncing on your knee,
your sweet baby waby
your sweet baby girl.

I love you
only as much as is required
to get my prize money
and trophy and get the
hell off this stage
so I can fling off this tutu
and these relentless shoes,
surrender to the solace
of drug-crashing sleep.

Swan

          re
G   y's
          A
       nat om   y
          as ori-
          gami.

The Biggest Loser

I am an obese woman
trapped in a slim woman's body.
My calorific intake is high,
but could be staggering.
I just need a scale, a TV crew,
and a support network.

I want to bite, chew, swallow
every minute of every day until
time ceases to exist.

I want to gorge on happiness
and unhappiness until I'm so absorbed by myself
I cannot move an inch.

I want to wear fat
like memory foam
and become my own indigestible dreams.

I want to roll my hunger
like dough and rise like a volcano
to the occasion.

I am an obese woman
trapped in a slim woman's body.
Look, my ribs are keys
of a player piano.
Look, look into my eyes,
fat as opera singers.

Survivor II: This Time It's Genocide

Poland is shot. And its wife. And its unborn child.
Revenge selects a deadlier arsenal of weapons.

Dictators appointed by agents construct arguments.
Hatreds rise like inflation and unemployment.
Gardens erect fences and tombstones.
Genetics punished by death squad.

Goodbye beautiful citizenship.
Perhaps you would like to trade your heirlooms for a loaf
of bread and slice of cheese.
Perhaps you would like to use a lifeline to warn your daughter
to stay silent in the attic or to trade costumes for the sake
of moving the plot along.

Each week, ten thousand campers are selected
for scientific experiment, ten thousand more must give up
the ghost.

The challenges get crueller. The prizes stranger.
The confessions more predictable.

Nations text their ballots into gas chambers,
go back to genetically modified climates
and genetically modified peace.

Funded entirely by product placement,
the fan website nearly crashes from all the orders
for little black mustaches, green cards, and souvenir stars.

ARGUMENTS

In the Library

In the map room
a new civilisation is surfacing.
Out of the drawers
a sun spills into a sea
a tower flies past a spaceship
a car gurgles a park.
If you would like to join us
we are meeting at midnight
at the microfiche
where our souls will be squeezed
through a viewfinder, photographed,
printed, & catalogued, so
no one forgets we were here
(before we disappear).

Let Me Bring You to the Brink

For at the brink, millimetres gain
sacred significance & the vertigo
I've suffered from for four years
suddenly has a place to sip her
martinis & call home.

I plant a handstand on the edge
of human existence tempting
mythical beasts to call my bluff,
make a scapegoat out of me,
or at the very least a media sensation.

When I was a little girl my father
& I would play Trivial Pursuit
for the privilege of copywriting
our current madness. I won three
winters of seasonal affective disorder.

When I stretch my gluttes & hams
at the end of a long training session,
I'm so relaxed in my immediate
surroundings I want to scream.
Compassion is a foreign movie

with fuzzy subtitles played to new
citizens waving tiny paper flags.
The brink is where lies are strangled
& the earth holds its final, deliberate,
patronising press conference.

Inside Out

The latest revolution produced
a curious side-effect.
Our bodies flipped inside out.

It's true, we eat with difficulty.
But what we eat is evident
to everyone & a successful
form of advertising.

Also, hospital wait times have
drastically decreased as doctors
filter less complaints
but are less revered now
that diseases are evident.

And we pick each other's brains
with ease and delight. Yesterday
I learned Serbian in seconds.

Curiously, though we literally
wear our hearts on our sleeves,
we are still no luckier in love.
Divorce rates have skyrocketed.
Restraining orders abound.

Even inside-out, the heart is an enigma.
We hire birds in hurt lockers
to detangle the veined fray.

Forward Thinking

Forward thinking is apparently better
Than backward thinking, or lateral thinking,
Or thinking standing on one's head
Or with hands tied behind one's back.

When we think forward, we think of moving
In a forward direction, and this directional motive
Is noble because it anticipates more forward
Motion in the future and momentum

Is everything. If you can think ahead of others,
Ahead of your cycle, ahead of your age,
You can arrive at the destination of thought –
The end – far more quickly than your contemporaries.

What will become of them? Oh, I suppose
They will fester in the thinking of yesteryear.
They will languish and lounge and sing songs
And eat things once called cherries or chocolates.

You will have better things to think about
Which will baffle friends and family. When you kiss
Wetness will already be left in the dust. When you hear
Watch Out – You Are Going To Be Hit By A

– you will have slammed into your own impact
A century ahead of schedule. Local community groups
Inevitably try to bury you. But, you have thought ahead.
The earth's orbit officially stamped outdated.

Advice for Burglars

I

If the house contains several shelves
of books, the stash squats in one of them:
Skip Shakespeare's *Sonnets* and the plays,
The Odyssey, *The Aeneid*, *War and Peace*.
Skip the tomes of national revolutions &
the vast encyclopedias, the dictionaries,
the Bibles, & the Qu'rans. Look
for the title that doesn't belong:
Accounting for Beginners or
The Grapefruit Diet –
there's your prize – a guaranteed
sham, the pages sliced, & buried
inside is the cash.

II

Don't forget
to make yourself a sandwich.
You're still a working man.

We Have Nothing Else to Say to Each Other

Aborted attempts at language instruction on 5 continents
my lips are sore with explications, declarations & awkward
apologies.

I present you with _____ .
You counter _____ .
Bow. Then back away from the table.

We worried once our phones were tapped, then realised
our blood was far ahead – technologically – in the betrayal market.
We laughed & pitched camp.
Those were good times & we printed souvenir t-shirts.

I felt close to you then.
Close to signing up for acupuncture & hypnotism
to decrease our dependence on life.

My god you were gorgeous in your prime.
Closed signs flipped to Open.
DVDs produced special features.
I brought you roses & rabies.

I entered an extreme downhill competition,
crashing into the 22nd century.

There, I tell you, my dialect destroys yours & I'm not sorry.
I'm a salesman, as usual, & the servants of sold-out syllables
set up shop like sullenly stupid star-struck lovers.

To My Suicidal Husband

Please do not look for poetry
in your death. Your drowning or
hanging or tsunami of pills & booze
will not be poetic.

There is no residue of poetry
in a bloated cheek snagged by a fish hook,
in a cracked leather belt swaying
from a light fixture or in a sludge of vomit
protruding from your throat like a second tongue.

And certainly no poetry will fall
upon your devastated wife folding
the last pairs of your dirty underwear &
ignoring the phone on a Saturday night,
piles of pizza crusts on the coffee table
one of your horror films running aimlessly
on the screen, wondering why you
never imagined her twitching hands,
the packing up of your extensive library,
or the signed book of your own poems,
To Priscila, my love, because nothing exists
without you, under her lumpy pillow, now
warm as soggy shoes left to dry in the sun, and
her sobbing the last of her suspect memories
of your tender eyes, your brisk, hunched
gait, the slow circling of your hands
across her belly, into the awful emptiness of
hangers, towels and toothbrush holders,
microwavable meals and refrigerator
reminders, because your imagination
failed to reconcile the oxymorons
of her & your death.

This is not poetry.
Trust me.

While I am still your wife, and not a warning.

There is nothing less poetic than your death.
And nothing more plain.

Who Will Bring You Breakfast When I'm Gone?

Who will bring you breakfast when I'm gone?
Who will butter your toast & know to butter your toast along the
        edges only?
Who will pour your orange juice & know to fill it right to the brim?
Who will brew your green tea with jasmine – & stew it long enough
so you forget you are drinking green tea with jasmine?
Who will scramble your eggs & flip them by telling dirty jokes?
Tell me who, who will do these, among other things, once I am gone?
And how am I to keep on living, knowing this?
How can I possibly be strong?

Epic Theory

Everyone wants to be the hero.
The man – or woman, let's not be rude –
who embarks on wild adventures,
earns boatloads of prizes,
sails triumphantly back home.

Everyone wants to be tight with the gods.
Or at least 'intimate', on a first name basis,
barring that, guided by their prickly hands,
no act completed without prior approval
and ephemeral lackeys counting scores.

Everyone wants an introduction and a conclusion.
A middle, an arc, a theme song.
For oracles' words to be worshipped as truth,
for birds and winds to be translated as signs.

Everyone wants a final chapter, a swan song,
a son or daughter to inherit
the tremulous future, a landscape of
fragrant flowers in which to fall and die.

But the majority perfect the chorus.
Nameless, androgynous, and masked,
out of danger and fame's way, mere echo
of what the crowd already thinks.

Teaching Is Becoming a Dangerous Profession

Pull out a book,
you might as well be pulling out
a grenade.

No one seems to recognise
what it is or how to use it
before it's too late.

The Professor of Nothing

He wakes at dawn with an idea
from a dream since evaporated
like steam on the bathroom mirror.

The lecture he prepared over fifteen hours
of intense indifference is over.
The theorem has mastered itself.

He shuts his empty briefcase and
heads to the conference room
for a muffin. He picks out
the raisins, and with a nostalgic pang
remembers that he likes raisins.

If he has a wife, she has a classical name.
He will move mountains in his spare
time to locate her and seize his prize,
once conclusions are forfeited and he can
sabbatical unburdened by the elements.

No Postcards

No postcards
of the stone pillar monument –
a rarity in war history –
in Quebec City dedicated to the memories
of both the winning and the losing sides.

Monctalm/Wolfe same type,
same block letters, French facing Chateau Frontenac
(the most photographed hotel in the world),
English facing the citadel of North America's
only remaining walled city.

No postcards either
of the abstract geometric sculpture
a gift to the city – only mentioned on walking tours
as an 'eyesore' – cubed shower stall a child
could have conceived: *Dialogue With History*.

In five days, I didn't see a single person go near it;
not even to laugh.

Maybe I'm not the person to be writing this poem.
I am the daughter of Trudeau – a double ethnic
who set up shop in Toronto, and spends as many winter
days as possible in Barbados, a specialist
in English literature.
Maybe this is none of my business.

But I want to buy postcards
of the Montcalm/Wolfe monument
and *Dialogue with History*.

No one can find me any.

Apparently, tourists don't write *wish you were here*
or *having a blast* or *missing you* on events
that forever changed the fortunes of North America.

And for anomalies like me digital cameras
capture the images if not the habitual disappointment one feels
encountering the past and not knowing how to care –
what to discard or keep or fortify. How to fit it all into
boxed shapes for strangers to ignore in the rolling darkness.

Identity Crisis

My cat thinks it's a dog.
My dog thinks it's a horse.
My horse thinks it's a car.
My car thinks it's a train.
My train thinks it's a submarine.
My submarine thinks it's a skyscraper.
My skyscraper thinks it's a museum.
My museum thinks it's a carnival.
My carnival thinks it's a funeral.
My funeral thinks it's a birth.
My birth thinks it's an episode.
My episode thinks it's eternal.
My eternal thinks it's hope.
My hope thinks it's cynicism.
My cynicism thinks it's time.
My time thinks it's an anachronism.
My anachronism thinks it's pride.
My pride thinks it's a cat.

The Penguin and the Flamingo

Like schoolchildren with barely enough time to register
the cold, greedy eyes of the fat bully on his way to claim
another's meagre treasure, the penguin and the flamingo
met on the road to Anywhere, shook wings, and decided right then
and there to indulge in a picnic. Both were toting instruments and
sang long laments about bygone eras and past loves into the night.

The penguin told of a world he had left with no cold.
The flamingo told of a world she had left with no heat.
The penguin's sweetheart had died of the water.
The flamingo's sweetheart had died of the air.

At least land survives, they agreed. Although both had been
set on the road to Anywhere for longer than they could count
by the remaining clouds or sun. After dessert – a pocketful
of flies – they were just about to dismantle camp and be on
their merry ways when a great wind whipped right through
their hearts and brains: *If you are both on the same road,
and this is the middle point, then Anywhere is here.*

The penguin and the flamingo began to dig.
Mine, mine! they yelled in unison.

The wind laughed, a hearty laugh that blew their beaks off.
Each refused to budge. Songs became a thing of yesteryear.
Memories of sweethearts grew dim as the light.

Eventually, the penguin shook off his tux.
Eventually, the flamingo shed her gown.

They hated each other by then, but made love anyway.
The sky sizzled with heat and cracked with cold.

Look for them on the road to Anywhere, Somewhere,
or Nowhere, wherever you happen to be, chasing tornados.

There Are No Time-outs in History

At best there are pauses between rounds
to stitch skin, wipe blood, spit into the bin,
& except for a few predictable platitudes,
collect bets & wave to what's left of the crowd.

RIDDLES

RSVP

A man sat drinking with his two ex-wives and his two sons and his two daughters, his spoiled stepsister and their two stepsons. The old man sat beside an uncle, a nephew at each arm. Only five people are at this picnic.

Answer: A redneck family reunion.
[Old answer: Lot and offspring.]

*

A Stranger Comes to Town

A creature sauntered by where many men sat hanging out – smart guys. He had one eye and two ears and two feet and twelve hundred heads, a back and belly and two hands, arms, and shoulder, plus one neck and two sides. What the hell is he?

Answer: An iPod salesman.
[Old answer: A one-eyed garlic pedlar.]

Coasting

My dress is silent on all subjects as I move over the earth and then rest in foreign waters. Sometimes I hike my skirt in the high air over soldiers' cabins and then I hightail it across the strong skies. My jewels twinkle loudly and I sing splendidly. When I am not relaxing on land or water, I wander, a ghost.

Answer: An airplane.
[Old answer: A swan.]

*

Extreme Eating Competition

Chewing words. Wondrous engine, regurgitates at our asking from dusk until dawn the infinite utterances of mankind. Interloper, we are none the wiser by the consumption.

Answer: Google.
[Old Answer: Moth.]

Battle of the Blades

I was a weapon, warrior. Now tough young bachelors cover me in gold and silver curves. Believe it or not, sometimes men kiss me. Sometimes I summon fights. Sometimes I'm smuggled over borders. Sometimes shipped over waters with bright trophies. Sometimes one of the guardians fills my cup with rings. Sometimes, it's awful – I must be brave, headless, and lie soiled, or be sanitised and strapped to walls where men drink. Sometimes, although rarely, warriors on mass lift and parade me through the streets. Most times I must fearlessly trap and recover possession of my voice from gangs of thieves. Take bets on my name.

Answer: Hockey stick.
[Old answer: Horn.]

*

UFC

I am whore of men; found growing wildly in groves and northern climes, plucked from the crevices of mountainsides. By day, I am treated with kids gloves, protected and sheltered. Later, hero, bathed in barrels. Now I am banger and beater – instantly I throw men to earth (predominantly lower class). Instantly, we discover who can hold his own and who will tough it out unless misguided coaching ceases not before. Drained of strength, speech deprived, he controls not his spirit, nor feet, nor fists. Ask for me at counters where foolish men nurse blows the morning after.

Answer: Red Bull.
[Old Answer: Mead.]

Recession

My house's foundation is in constant flux, yet I do not protest our mutual venture. I am speedier than you, often more muscular – but you are more enduring. Sometimes I am sluggish and stagnant, while you rush carelessly forward. Tied to your strings, even as I await mergers. Until death do us part.

Answer: Stock Market.
[Old Answer: Fish in the stream.]

*

Vicious Cycle

Abandoned for dead, barely begun to live. Assigned a foster mother, who clothed and fed me with the same kindness she showed her biological children. As was my destiny, I swelled with milk from her breasts, among strangers. She kept feeding me and feeding me and I grew up big and strong, seeking violent adventures. Soon, my new mother had fewer sons and daughters to call her own.

Answer: Death row inmate.
[Old Answer: Cuckoo.]

DEFENCES

The Delicate Synthesis

Let me tell you a story: Once upon a time
a big-haired woman with clouds for a dress
opened her mouth & rocks rolled out.
Giant rocks tumbled onto giant rocks &
thus were hills & mountains formed.
Then these hills & mountains in turn
opened their mouths – to sing the big-
haired woman's praises, of course – &
more rocks tumbled out & thus cities
& temples formed.

         Look out: one day, a soreness
         will grab you, a heavy-headed ache,
         & you too will open your mouth &
         a giant rock will tumble out:
         For millennia, this big-haired woman
         with clouds for a dress has been
         lovingly planning your tombstone.
         You will sign it with a cough &
         the story will begin over again.

In Defence of the Canon

I would have been interested in Henry Fielding
as a man, yes, as a man, regardless of his pretensions
& his marrying a chambermaid. I would have eaten
large poultry meals with him then licked his throat.

& Sidney I would have seduced out on the battlefield
in my naughty nurse outfit. I would have said, *My Lord,
let me take your temperature*, & occasioned a sonnet
sequence premiered at court. What a tragedy he died
so young that I have only his portrait to covet.

& Donne, well, there is no doubt I would have swooned, panted,
crawled into his confessional for repentance, admitting
to compulsive horrific deeds just to hear him gasp.

& Stein, I could have been her flapper mistress trading Freudian slips
over cryptic crosswords and 2000 piece jigsaw puzzles.

I'd have curled up with Calvino too, on a night train to the ends
of the world, offering myself up like the happiest whore. & out the
                caboose
we'd shoot the history of thoughts of dead writers. Love tumbling
out like syllables. Two halves of the brain closing like a book.

Rilke and I exchange emails

He in his castle & me in my basement
we send each other short updates
on our mental travels, prescription advice,
& religious jokes.

We never post or discuss poetry.
Every three months we change
our passwords & must guess
via subject headlines based on
past correspondence.

My therapist says this is called
an emotional affair & I should come clean
to my partner about it. But I respect
Rilke's fame & want to keep our
records to ourselves.

Notoriety precipitates secrets
& short form. Today he forwards a recipe
for removing wine stains. I solicit aid
with my crossword. I can't think of
a five-letter word for everlasting life.

I've Stopped Counting Calories

Instead, I've replaced my morning ritual
with counting hairs on my pillow, steam lines
on the bathroom mirror, the number of citizens
against ceasefire in the Middle East on the comments
section of the morning Post.

I count children wearing iPods, grown men
in plaid cotton shorts on the subway, old women
with hair ribbons, how many bulldozers it takes
to fix a mile of streetcar tracks.

In the afternoon, I count the number of 'likes'
overheard in an hour, candy wrappers
dropped in sewers, MRI appointments, flushes
in washrooms in our city alone.

I note loafers vs. sneakers, natural gas vs. electrical,
truck traffic over the border, rainbows this side
of the equator.

In the evening, I pinpoint neon lights,
prostitutes without mittens, drivers on cellphones,
clouds bemoaning the lack of blue sky to call home.

Then I call you.
And you count the times I've dreamed of your smile.

I multiply by ten.
Divide by three.
Add the year.

And send you my love as fast as it takes us to burn a single calorie.
By our breathing alone.

I've lost the ability to feel pain

I've lost the ability to feel pain
& life is simpler.
This morning I sliced off my neighbour's
head, stole into his dining room & danced
a marathon.
My limbs accessories, I choose
whether to put them on.
My frown merely a fetish.
I sleep on brass nails & phone my in-laws.
I stick artefacts into orifices just to see
what happens.
I follow the trail to a point
then get bored.

My pain sent me an express post
message a month ago:

Without you life ceases to have meaning.
Without me life ceases.

I think he has it all backwards, as usual.
My pain is masculine.
(No surprise.)

I used to disguise my pain in frilly
dresses, champagne cocktails
& graduate diplomas.
What an expensive habit!

My bank balance, since rebounded,
likes to taunt my pain, tempting it
into midnight roulette matches.
(My bank balance is also masculine.)

I'm waiting for my pain to get seriously
sick so I can prepare salves & salty soups
& pay it the avid attention it once gave me.
I'll tuck it in a blue blanket
& sing it lullabies.

I can sing. Now that I don't
feel pain, I have developed
a wider vocal range
and am always in tune.

I Sold My Future Life on eBay

I'd been hoping for at least two million –
enough for my present life to retire on the south coast
of Barbados, banana daiquiris morning, noon, and
night, and my own private catamaran from which
to torment the tropical fish.

A bidding war ensued, but uncertainty finally
deterred even the most salient and most reckless. No guarantees
of a happy life, a long life, a productive life. No transferable
memories or DNA or religious inclinations. No geographical
or historical or sexual preferences accommodated.
Just one life out of billions.

Once you've been assigned a body, of course, it's more
difficult to give up, no matter the dreary circumstances.
But to pay for a life and it not live up to expectations – criminal.
Who has the heart for such disappointment?

A frugal few, hedging their bets, are in the business
of hoarding future lives. As of midnight, mine appears on their list.
Not really what I imagined when I prepped the post,
but there's nothing I can do about that now. *C'est la vie.*

I might end up tucked away in a storage locker or downloaded
by a sweaty stockbroker. I might end up in my beloved Caribbean
on a ten-speed or spraying pesticides in a weed-riddled backyard.

At least I can take comfort in the knowledge
I orchestrated my own shaky auction, circumventing deeds
of the old masters, who bought and sold us, bought and sold us,
without a thought to our futures, body or soul.

Fortress

A lion brings a cobra to the picnic.
Eighteenth-century ladies wipe their brows
with EU flags. The universe is up
in a code red tither, the planets
slamming their doors.
                    Exactitude: word
of the day. Tantrum: master of the soul.
The earth's area rug extends past the lunar
landscape, past the holes in the ozone,
past particle memory, to where our DNA
curls up, asleep.

Bodies polluted like lakes.
Can't you see my breasts stuffed
with seaweed, my frontal lobe liquefied
by salt? Morning electrocutions proceed
on schedule, the clouds botox their cheeks
and keep smiling.
                    Deep in the gut
of the new millennium, amazing graces
are sanctioned like cigars. We await
the arrival of zillions of more babies,
while a large man with a bass tone
breaks plate after plate against
the force field of mankind.

Why Would Anyone Go Back to Brazil Under These Circumstances?

I didn't leave my mother there.
I didn't leave my lover there.
I didn't leave my belongings there.
I didn't leave my heart there.

I didn't leave my sanity there.
I didn't leave my compassion there.
I didn't leave my trust there.
I didn't leave my intelligence there.

I didn't leave my god there.
I didn't leave my nationality there.
I didn't leave my ethnicity there.
I didn't leave my name there.

I didn't leave my home there.
I didn't leave my second home there.
I didn't leave my mind there.
I didn't leave my death there.

I didn't leave there.
I didn't leave there.
I didn't leave there.
I didn't leave there.

An Exercise in Recovering Your Inner Child

Priscila, it still stings to have no mother and
father's legs remain eternally useless no matter
how many pleas you make to God or how firm
your resolve to remain a virgin until they are returned.
You will cease, in time, hiding in closets pretending
to be invisible or scrapbooking dandelions to save them
from lawnmowers, but you will continue to bite your nails and
love men who sometimes scare you with their despair. Thankfully,
you will give up your aspirations to be a world class pianist and
wetting the bed. Visions of the Virgin Mary & the assault
of crab apples against windowpanes will wane during storms.
Your dreams will evolve into more precise categories and
you will learn the art of deflection and fill your allotted space
with rescued cats and books, the way you always knew you
would, even as the motorbike revs that will scar your left leg
for life (half-moon print of a pointless puncture) and send you
peddling home with the dull pain of pointless anger, eyelashes
falling one by one on the gravel road to where, intermittently,
on days where you are gratefully ignored, it feels like something
your gut calls home. *They'll grow back, my dear!* I promise.
Whether you want them to or not. *They'll grow back!*

Magdalene Desires

My effort is clandestine: to locate you
in the remotest places of our darkness, groping

for a hand, a piece of leg, the puncture of a
rib, and mould it to my spine like your long

ledgers that detail my famous sins,
forgiveness, pre-forced acts, love bites,

and over by the tall brick walls
where our names rest and the golden

calf crouches like an anguished animal, unsure
of slaughter but suspecting its assault over

the horizon with the first clanging of the bell
tower.
         My nerves rattle like a snake you invented
to amuse the children, its hypnotising dance

the proud parade of a long line of witnesses,
shedding skins at break of day. It is cooler

in other countries, this motion for which we
give many names, this forward spiral, unentered

entry, vast well of clear forbidden water.
Bless me. I've no pride, nor confidence to speak

of you to my family or friends. Meet me
when I least expect you. Wear my favourite perfume.

I will prostrate myself, and you will know me
like a stone smoothed to shape by an eager hand.

Books *Do* Hold Me at Night

As I open my eyes in the morning, so do books.
Eat breakfast, lunch, dinner and dessert at my side.
Amuse on subways, trains, and planes.
Hold my tongue in meetings and during the news.
Take my temperature when I'm feverish.
Grieve when I'm sad.

I've had orgasms with books, alone and in unison.
Travelled to the ends of the earth.
Teetered on the edge of pools and baths.
Waited patiently in cafés for my safe return.
Stayed tight to the chest in the dark.

Books dressed me during puberty.
Held their own at university.
Knew before I did that *he* and *he* and *she* were not the one.
Stood quietly aside while my babies were born.
Sometimes beat me senseless.

Books sweat with me on the elliptical.
Idle on summer porches.
Recognise my neighbours and crawl
into my children's hands.
Treasure old memories more fondly
than I do.

Books are survivors.
Change hats: father to uncle, daughter to professor.
Harness the crowd. Rewire the individual.
Know when to hit the brakes, when to bet the highest stakes.
I even believe, though you insist otherwise,
you know how to die.

And now that we're on the subject.
My most loyal companions, I leave you
all my worldly and unworldly possessions.
Build a castle out of our pages.
Trust no one. Beware of fire.

I Spent My Savings on Salvation

& what I've got left is
a banana-coloured bikini, two unwritten memoirs,
& a suffering-of-the-month subscription.

I rode the bus because the Devil
told me it would be more Catholic & now my neck
aches & I can't lift my legs higher than a shuffle.

Every day I race
a cramped x-sport speedway on stolen skates –
crashing into bad decisions,
traumatic memories & the untold confessions
of my misguided, thrill-seeking soul.

In the collection plate I drop
diamonds, diatribes, and diabetes.
I gain more loyal followers from the diamonds,
but what-to-do? I'm a Marxist at heart,
though I channel champagne
& elitism through my chakras.

Economies mutate numbers.
I trample my mind with avalanche terror & then throw $ at it.
My advisor promises prime bankruptcy-protection rates.

I love you soul,
& not for your $.

The Happy Genius of Our Household

In our cellar, underneath the tomato plants,
we keep a key, a tiny key
of silver paint.

If anyone else knew we had this key,
we'd be toast, we'd be on the lam,
we'd be fugitives, we'd need witness protection,
we'd be elected officials.

If you hold the key up to a skylight
you can witness your own birth.
If you tilt this key slightly to the left
you will come in your pants.
But the real trick of the key is to go up,
go up, into the future.

We don't need the key now, but I'm so glad it's there,
growing comfortable and complacent in the corner
with the trusty tomatoes.

For the key to the future is an emergency procedure.
If you squeeze before it's time
you will turn into a jury of your peers.
And the birds will use the key to unlock your grave.

Serendipity

Were I invited to name a planet
(& why not?), such a globe in the universe
would be called *Serendipity*. We would live there.

We'd wake to the smell of Colombian coffee
engage in Chinese calisthenics before
a rodizio lunch
siesta then squaredance
read old Russian novels while
sipping champagne &
throat-sing into the night.

Our flag would be a bird without borders.
Our anthem composed by shooting our names out
of a canon & catching the rain.

We would speak only when absolutely necessary
& in oxymorons.

Work days & holidays indistinguishable.
My mother = my sister = my grandfather =
my long lost neighbour = my hairdresser.

Every object in our homes native & artifact.

We would dream all possible permutations
of planet, animals, & species. & each
would be a paragon of you.

The Day the World Ends
a found poem

Leave all purses and other personal belongings.
Line up against the right wall,
women and children first.
Check under the door for signs of heat or smoke.
If clear, walk in single file.
Do not use elevators.
Walk out of the building to a place of safety.

If heat or smoke is evident, block the outlet.
Open a window if one is available.
Do not try to be a hero.
Wait calmly for assistance.
Do not panic.

FOOTNOTE

Nine Lives

He thought he heard his mother's voice over the telephone wire.

*

The carpet cleaner might have been better stored under lock and key.

*

Tested Theory: A cat will always land on his feet.

*

He gave it away happily to Esmeralda.

*

The wily fox sported a new fur. The intended thought she would try it on for size.

*

A bathtub, a birthday card, a cinnamon bun, a gold necklace, a hung jury.

*

All that jazz, baby. Cool cats and a howl gone wrong.

*

He'd exploited the waffle maker, his buddies insisted, with the best of intentions.

*

The white light inside the eyes shimmered across the continent and set sail for home.

ACKNOWLEDGEMENTS

Previous versions of these poems were published in the following magazines and anthologies: *A Crystal Through Which Love Passes: Glosas for P.K. Page* (ed. Jessie Ferguson), *Arc Poetry Magazine, carte blanche, Catch Up* (US), *Canadian Journal of Environmental Education: Special Issue on Art, Literature, and Place: An Ecopoetics Reader, Descant, The HarperCollins Book of English Poetry by Indians* (Sudeep Sen, editor), *The Mackinac Poetry Magazine* (US), *The Malahat Review, New Orleans Review* (US), *Other Tongues: Mixed Race Women Speak Out* (ed. Adebe DeRango-Adem & Andrea Thompson), *Ottawater, The Poetry Foundation* (Chicago), *Prism International, Rogue Stimulus: The Stephen Harper Holiday Anthology for a Prorogued Parliament* (ed. Stephen Brockwell & Stuart Ross), *The Same* (US), *South-Asian Ensemble, Studio, The Warwick Review* (UK), and *The Yellow Nib: Contemporary English Poetry By Indians* (Queen's University Belfast, ed. Sudeep Sen). Many thanks to all the editors.

Many thanks, as well, to Neil Astley, for his continued support in introducing my work to international audiences and all the amazing wizardry he does on the behalf of poetry. Thank you, as well, to my fellow poet traveller Tishani Doshi, and all festival and reading series organisers in Britain and Ireland who participated in the Bloodaxe poetry tour we took in April and May of 2013, including Cúirt International Literature Festival, Hull Central Library Reading Series, Liverpool International Poetry Festival, Newcastle Centre for the Literary Arts, Scottish National Library Reading Series, International Lyric Poetry Festival Sheffield, and the Wordsworth Trust Poetry Series. Thank you for fulfilling a dream of mine to read poetry at Wordsworth's cottage in Grasmere and beyond.

And never lastly, thank you to my love and constant companion, Christopher Doda, who rarely bats an eye at any word I say or write, and always believes.